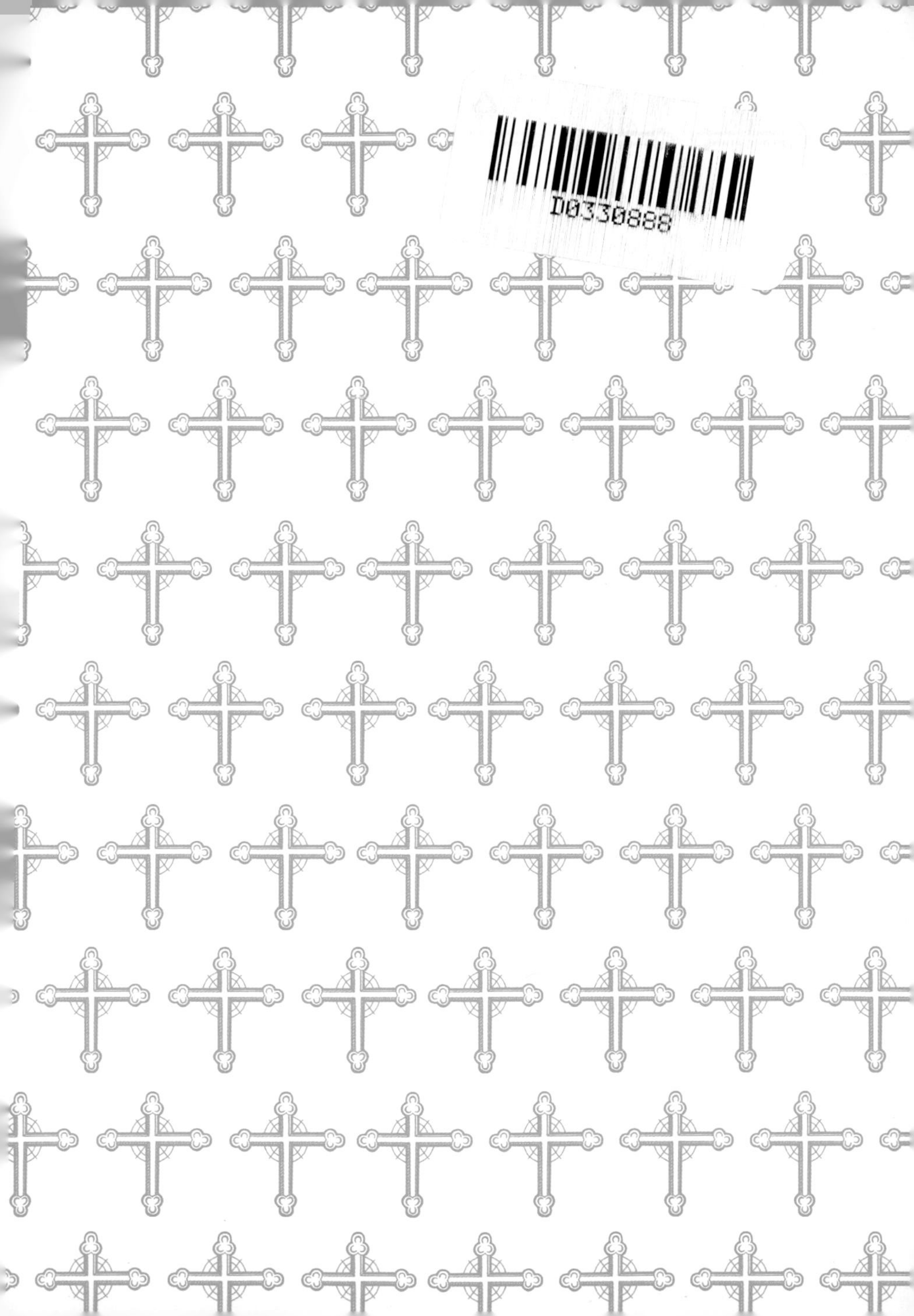

SAINTS FOR GIRLS
"HEROINES OF GOD"

BY

DANIEL A. LORD, S.J.

1946 EDITION

NIHIL OBSTAT
JOHN M. FEARNS, S.T.D.

IMPRIMATUR
+ FRANCIS CARDINAL SPELLMAN, *Archbishop, New York*

CUM PERMISSU SUPERIORUM

Manufactured in Hong Kong through InterPress Ltd.
December 2012 --- Job# 121027

St. Agatha

THE PURE VIRGIN

Saint Agatha was very beautiful. People looked at her and said, "Oh, she is the fairest girl alive."

But Agatha was also very pure and good.

She loved Jesus Christ very much. She promised God she would never marry. "All my love is Yours," she said. "I will live and die for You."

Now it happened that the Governor of Sicily where Agatha lived heard of her beauty.

So he sent for her. Soldiers came and arrested her.

"You are a Christian," they said. "So you must go to jail."

"Dear Lord Jesus," she prayed, "I belong to You. Do not let this tyrant have power over me."

He made love to her. But she refused him.

So he threw her into prison. The governor was sure Agatha would be so afraid of prison that she would consent to love him.

Instead, she made the wicked woman who was her jailer love God too.

So the Governor ordered her to be tortured. She was not afraid. Then he ordered her to be beaten.

"Dear Jesus," she cried, "come and take me."

And Jesus came and took her home to heaven.

Her Feast is February 5th.

St. Agnes

THE LITTLE MARTYR

Agnes was only twelve when the Roman soldiers arrested her.

They were killing all Christians in those days. But first they dragged her to the statue of a false goddess.

Offer prayers and incense to Minerva," they ordered her.

Instead, brave little Agnes lifted her arms and prayed aloud to Jesus Christ.

So they put handcuffs on her. She was so tiny that the cuffs slipped off her wrists.

Then they whipped her cruelly. They said they would stop if she gave up Jesus Christ. Even the pagans wept to see her tortured that way.

Next they dragged her through the streets for the people to laugh at. Instead, some of them tried to save her.

Then a young man asked her to marry him.

"I will save you if you do," he promised.

I belong to my Savior alone," she answered.

With one stroke of the sword, the soldiers killed this brave little girl.

Her Feast is January 21st.

St. Angela

FRIEND OF GIRLS

Angela de Merici was a lovely young Italian woman. She knew many poor girls.

Most of them did not know about Jesus Christ.

Many of them had never heard much about the lovely Mother of God.

Many of them were sinful and bad. But Angela knew this was because no one had taught them to be good.

So she gathered children around her and taught them about Jesus and Mary.

She helped sinful girls to become good once more.

She built houses where they could live and be safe from temptation.

She found fine, pure, wise young women to teach the children. She wanted sinless girls to help save sinful girls. She took Saint Ursula for her patron.

Then she invited good young women and pure, sweet girls to help her.

They became the first Ursuline Sisters.

They went all over the world teaching and helping little children and girls and young women.

Today there are thousands of these Sisters. They all call Saint Angela their Patroness and Holy Mother.

Her Feast is January 27th.

St. Ann

MOTHER OF THE BLESSED VIRGIN

Ann was a dear old lady who had been married a long time.

But God had never sent her a child. That made her sad.

She wanted a baby to brighten her home. She kept praying to God, and God heard her prayer.

Her lovely little baby was Mary.

But even her happy Mother did not know that this little girl would be the Mother of God.

Ann gave her daughter the best home she could. She sent her to school in the Temple. She loved her very much.

All the time, God knew Ann would be the Grand-mother of His Son.

Because she was so good to Mary, His Mother, Jesus made Ann a great saint.

When we pray to her, we know that Jesus, her Grandson, will listen to what she asks for us.

Her Feast is July 26th.

St. Barbara

THE BRAVE MARTYR

When Barbara was a little girl, her wicked father imprisoned her in a high tower.

So Barbara lived in the tower with only the servants who cared for her. And she was very good.

One day a priest passed under her tower. He was singing about Jesus Christ. Barbara heard him. She asked him about his song. He told her all about the Savior. Barbara was overjoyed.

"I love Jesus too," she cried. "I am a Christian."

When her father heard this, he was furious.

In those days, it was against the law to love Jesus or to be a Christian. So this cruel father dragged his own daughter to the judge.

"My daughter is a Christian," he cried. "She is not my daughter any longer."

"What shall we do with her?" the judge asked. For he saw that Barbara was good and pure.

"Do what the law orders," her father shouted. "Beat her until she is almost dead. Then chop off her head."

So the soldiers carried out that cruel order.

But suddenly they saw angels coming. The angels carried the soul of Barbara to heaven. And a terrible flash of lightning struck her cruel father and killed him where he stood.

Her traditional Feast is December 4th.

St. Bernadette

THE LITTLE SAINT OF LOURDES

Bernadette's mother and father were very poor.

One day Bernadette went to gather firewood. She came to a cave near a flowing river. Her friends played and sang. But Bernadette stood still, her eyes wide with wonder.

For she saw a beautiful Lady, who was dressed in blue and white. There were stars around the Lady's head. Roses were on her feet. Bernadette told her parents and friends. At first they did not believe her.

But Bernadette saw the lovely Lady again and again. The lovely Lady ordered her to dig. A fresh, cool spring came bubbling up out of the ground.

Sick people who bathed in it grew well. Many of the blind could see again.

"Build here," said the lovely Lady, "a great church. And tell people to pray and do penance and walk in processions."

They did all this. Soon the wonderful Shrine of Lourdes was built.

And Bernadette waited until after the Lady had made her last visit to her. Then she went into the convent. She became a nun.

All the world knows about Lourdes. It is a beautiful shrine of Our Lady.

Her traditional Feast is February 18th.

St. Brigid

THE IRISH NUN

When Brigid was a very little girl, Saint Patrick converted the Irish. She was a very beautiful little girl. Many young men wanted to marry her.

I shall be a nun," she thought. But she never knew she was going to be the first of millions of Irish nuns throughout the world.

"Make me ugly," she prayed to God. "Then I can love You alone."

God heard her prayer and she became very ugly.

With joy she became a sister, a nun. And as soon as she did, God made her more beautiful than ever.

She built a lovely little convent. She tended the cattle herself. Other young women heard about her. They came and asked to join her and be nuns too.

Then little girls came to be taught.

The sick came to her and asked her to care for them.

Often she sold everything she had and gave the money to the poor.

So the Irish called on her for help from all over the country.

So all over Ireland she went. She built convent schools and hospitals everywhere.

And when she died, all Ireland loved her. They made her the Patroness of the Green Isle.

Her Feast is February 1st.

St. Catherine Of Siena

THE RESTORER OF THE POPE IN ROME

Catherine of Sienna was one of the greatest women that ever lived. When she was a little girl, our dear Lord appeared to her.

"Please give me your heart," He asked.

She gave it willingly. Jesus gave her His Sacred Heart in return.

Many rich young men wanted to marry this beautiful girl.

Instead, she became a Dominican Sister.

In those days, the Pope did not live in Rome. He had moved to France. Catherine went to see him.

"Holy Father," she said, "your place is in Rome. Come home to your people."

The Pope obeyed this simple little nun.

Many of the princes were furious. They did not want the Pope in Rome. So they tried to elect a false Pope.

Catherine, without fear, told them this was wrong. They were afraid of her. They listened and obeyed.

The Pope knew she was very wise, and often asked for her advice. She always told him just what Jesus wanted and what would please God.

Although she was only thirty-three when she died, the whole world knew this saintly girl. They loved this brave woman.

Her Feast is April 29th.

SUZANNE
COLLINS
KACEY
MUSGRAVES
CLUTCH POWERS
FROZEN
DELUXE EDITION
BRUNO MARS
UNORTHODOX JUKEBOX
No ads
No waiting
No late fees

St. Cecilia

THE MUSICIAN

Cecilia was a lovely Roman girl. She loved Jesus with all her heart.

But a young Roman wanted to marry her. She told him she belonged to Our Lord alone. At first he and his brother were very angry. They tried to force marriage on her.

But when the young man walked toward Cecilia, he saw her strong, beautiful Guardian Angel standing at her side.

The young man at once became a Christian. So did his brother.

The Roman soldiers came and took all three of them prisoners.

They cried, "Offer sacrifice to our gods."

But Cecilia, though just a young woman, spoke for all of them.

"We love and serve only the true God." she answered.

So all three went to Heaven together in martyrdom.

Just a few years ago, Cecilia's body was found in its grave in Rome. Though she had been dead for almost eighteen hundred years, her body was still fresh and sweet and beautiful as if she were asleep. Thus God protects those who love Him.

Her Feast is: November 22nd.

IHS

St. Cecilia

THE MUSICIAN

Cecilia was a lovely Roman girl. She loved Jesus with all her heart.

But a young Roman wanted to marry her. She told him she belonged to Our Lord alone. At first he and his brother were very angry. They tried to force marriage on her.

But when the young man walked toward Cecilia, he saw her strong, beautiful Guardian Angel standing at her side.

The young man at once became a Christian. So did his brother.

The Roman soldiers came and took all three of them prisoners.

They cried, "Offer sacrifice to our gods."

But Cecilia, though just a young woman, spoke for all of them.

"We love and serve only the true God." she answered.

So all three went to Heaven together in martyrdom.

Just a few years ago, Cecilia's body was found in its grave in Rome. Though she had been dead for almost eighteen hundred years, her body was still fresh and sweet and beautiful as if she were asleep. Thus God protects those who love Him.

Her Feast is: November 22nd.

IHS

St. Clare

FRANCISCAN NUN OF THE POOR

Sometimes we call her Saint Clare. Sometimes, Saint Clara or Saint Claire.

Her mother and father were very rich. She lived in a beautiful Italian palace.

But she listened to a man named Saint Francis of Assisi. He was very like Christ. He loved God. He wanted to be poor. He hoped to save the world from sin.

So, when her parents said she could not be a nun, Clare ran away. She cut her hair. She put on old clothes with a rope for her belt. In a little hut, she took her sister, then her mother and some friends. She began the sisters known as the Poor Clares.

All day long these sisters pray for sinners. They love God for those who do not love Him. They do penance so that men and women will not lose their souls.

Once the army of men who hated Christ came to Assisi. They meant to destroy the city.

Saint Clare carried the Blessed Sacrament outside the convent. Only her sisters were around her. But the great army saw her coming. They turned and fled in panic.

She had saved the city.

Her Feast is August 11th

St. Colette

THE BRAVE NUN

Colette lived in dangerous times.
Three men all pretended to be the real Pope.
Many Christians did not know which was the true Pope. But Colette did.
When she was a little girl she became a sister.
Saint Francis appeared to her in a vision one day. He asked her to love God very much.
"And make your sisters good nuns," he begged her.
So she did. She showed them how happy a good nun is. She taught them how to take care of the poor and teach little children about Jesus Christ.
This little nun loved the Catholic Church very much.
So God showed her which was the right Pope.
Bravely she told the Bishops and Cardinals what to do. They followed her advice. One Pope was elected and the Church was happy again.
The devils hated her because she was so good. They feared her because she loved the Church.
So they appeared to her in ugly shapes. They played horrid tricks on her. They tempted her severely.
"Stop praying to Jesus," they cried, "and we will stop bothering you." But she only prayed the harder.
She died smiling as she was praying to God to forgive all sinners.
Her Feast is March 6th.

St. Dorothy

THE GIRL MARTYR

Dorothy's Mother and Father had both been martyrs.

They had bravely died for Jesus Christ.

So the soldiers came for the little girl too. They dragged her to the judge. They beat and punished her. But she was faithful to Christ.

The judge told two wicked women to take her and show her how silly it was to believe in Our Lord. Instead, she converted them and made them both Christians.

The judge was now furious. He ordered the soldiers to treat her more cruelly. She only smiled. She did not think of her pain but of the two souls she had saved.

It was mid-winter when she was put to death. There was no fruit and no flowers. A pagan lawyer who hated Christ laughed at her.

"Send me some apples or roses from Heaven, will you?" he asked.

Just before she died, a little child stood at her side with three apples and three roses. The child was an angel from Heaven.

"Take them to the lawyer," Dorothy smiled and died.

The lawyer too became a Catholic and died a martyr.

Her traditional Feast is February 6th.

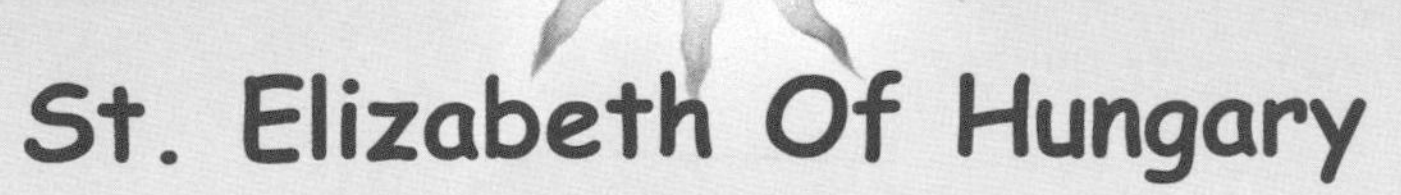

St. Elizabeth Of Hungary

FEEDER OF THE POOR

St. Elizabeth, Queen of Hungary, was only twenty-four when she died.

But what a beautiful life she had led!

Her father was a king. Her aunt was St. Hedwig.

When she was very young, she married Louis, a young nobleman, who soon became king.

She was sweet to her husband and loved her children. But she knew that queens should be very good to the poor and the sick. So she took care of them in the palace. She nursed them in the hospitals.

Her husband grew angry. "That's no work for a queen," he said.

One day she went to visit the poor. Her cloak was full of provisions. Her husband met her.

"Are you carrying food like a servant?" he cried.

He pulled open her cloak. Out fell not food but lovely red and white roses. Her husband asked her forgiveness. He knew she was a saint.

Her husband died when she was still very young. The next king treated her very badly and threw her out of her palace.

But she trusted God and God took her swiftly to His palace in Heaven.

Her Feast is November 17th.

St. Frances Of Rome

THE HELPER

Frances was a married saint.

She had always wanted to be a nun. But her parents wouldn't let her. They insisted she marry a wealthy Roman nobleman.

Once she was married, Frances and her husband lived forty years without a hard word or unkind deed. She was a good wife and a saintly mother.

Yet she prayed all she could. She took care of the poor, giving them even her own food. But she knew her chief duty was to take care of her house. Even prayer came second to that.

Then her troubles came. The enemies of her country captured Rome. They stole her property. They drove her husband away. They threw her son into prison. Frances was very poor. But she accepted all this as God's will.

When peace was restored, Frances started a new order of nuns.

Then her husband died. And Frances joined the nuns herself.

Often she saw her own guardian angel. When she was very good, his light was very bright. If she committed even a fault, his light faded away.

Her Feast is March 9th.

St. Genevieve

THE LITTLE SHEPHERDESS

Like Saint Joan of Arc, little Genevieve was a shepherdess. She tended her sheep near Paris.

One day a great saint passed by. He saw the little girl. "She is very holy," he said. "She will grow holier still." She spent her time in praying, in caring for the sick, in helping the poor.

A powerful king attacked Paris. The people were starving. Little Genevieve, quite unafraid, took some of her girl friends, and went out where the enemy could see her. They gathered food and brought it back to, the starving Parisians. No one dared to hurt her.

Another time, another general attacked Paris.

"Join with me in praying and fasting," she cried to the people. "He will not hurt us or hurt the city."

Everyone in Paris did as she said. To their delight, the general and his army packed up and left the city unharmed.

The new King of France had just become a Catholic.

Clovis was his name.

He heard about Genevieve and sent for her.

"Teach me how to be a good king," he asked this little shepherdess.

Paris loved Saint Genevieve. She is the city's patroness.

Her Feast is January 3rd.

St. Gertrude

THE MYSTIC

Sometimes men and women are so holy that Our Dear Lord comes to talk with them.

He likes to bring His Blessed Mother with Him too.

And they both tell these saints about Heaven and about the things the Holy Family did on earth.

Gertrude was a saint like this.

She was a holy nun who lived in a convent in Germany.

She was very clever. When she was a little girl she could write and speak Latin. But most of all, she wanted to know about God. So often Our Dear Lord and His Mother appeared to her.

They told her lovely secrets about life after death. They told her how safely we can all reach Heaven.

All these things Saint Gertrude wrote down in lovely books. We can still read these books.

How sweet it is to be very holy. For then Christ and Mary love to be with us.

Her Feast is November 16th.

St. Helen

FINDER OF JESUS' CROSS

Helen was a British princess. She became Empress of Rome.

At first, she was not a Christian. But she was a good woman. So soon Our Lord gave her the gift of faith.

Her strongest son was named Constantine. He was a pagan too. But when he saw his Mother become a Christian, he started thinking.

When Helen was eighty years old, she went to Jerusalem. She wanted to find the Cross on which Our Lord died.

She found three crosses buried in Mount Calvary. But when the Cross of Our Lord touched a very sick woman, at once the woman was cured.

Later, Helen's son was fighting his strongest enemy. He remembered the Cross his Mother loved. He promised to become a Christian if he won.

He did win. And the Cross became the sign of victory for all the world.

So Saint Helen by her prayers and example made her son, Constantine, the first Christian ruler of the world.

Her traditional Feast is August 18th.

St. Jane Frances De Chantal

LOVER OF GOD

Here is a wonderful saint.

She was a saint as a little girl. She was a saint as a wife. When she was a widow, she was a saint. Then she became a nun and was a saint in the convent.

When she was a very little girl, Jane Frances asked Our Lady to take care of her. Our Lady always did.

Then she married a nobleman. She made him a beautiful home. She loved her husband. She was devoted to her children.

But sorrow came to her. Her good husband died. Two children and a sister died. Her friends bothered her to marry again. She was sad and her life was very hard.

At last her children grew up. She knew that God wanted her to be a nun. So with Saint Francis de Sales she started the Visitation Order.

Her daughters, the Visitation Sisters, to this day pray, do penance, and teach children to love and serve God as Jane Frances did.

Her Feast is August 18th.

Jhesus
Maria

St. Joan Of Arc

THE GIRL SOLDIER

Joan of Arc did not start out to be a soldier. She was just a simple little shepherd girl.

She lived quietly in France with her family. But she loved God very much. And she wanted to see her country free and strong.

At that time, her country was fighting the English. The English were winning everywhere.

Suddenly Joan heard the voices of angels and saints speaking to her. "Go and save your country," they commanded her.

At first she was afraid. But then she knew God wished it. So she wore armor and rode a horse into battle.

The poor French king had not even his crown. The armies were afraid.

But Joan led them to victory. She crowned the king in his own palace. Then she said, "My work is done. Let me go back to my sheep."

But the king would not let her. Instead, her friends let the enemy capture her. And they burned her to death at the stake.

Joan's soul went straight to God. Her work was done. The French had won their country back.

And Joan is the patroness of soldiers who fight for their land.

Her Feast is: May 30th.

St. Julia

VIRGIN MARTYR

Julia was a rich noblewoman. She lived in North Africa.

The armies that hated Christ captured her country. Julia was seized and sold as a slave.

A rich merchant bought her. So this sweet, gentle, well educated woman did the hardest work of his house without pay. But she smiled and was brave. She prayed constantly to Jesus whom she loved.

Some time later, her master took her to a pagan place where people were praying to false gods.

Julia refused to have part in it.

One of the rich Romans was furious. He cried out, "That slave girl is a Christian. She should die." Her owner protected her.

But when her owner was asleep, the Roman seized her.

"Pray to my gods," he cried. "I will set you free if you do."

"Everyone is free," she answered, "if they love, Jesus Christ."

So the Roman beat her, nailed her to a cross, and she died a saint and martyr.

Her Feast is May 23rd.

St. Lucy

THE EYE SAINT

When Lucy was a little girl in Italy, her Mother was very ill.

"Let's pray," said Lucy, "and I know you'll get well."

So they prayed at the little church of Saint Agatha in Rome. Suddenly Saint Agatha appeared to Lucy. "Lucy, my sister!" she said to the little girl; "your Mother will be well. But you will die a martyr for Christ."

Next morning, her Mother was well.

Lucy was very rich. In gratitude she gave her money to the poor. Then she became a nun.

It happened that a young man who did not believe in Christ loved Lucy. He wanted her to marry him. When he heard she was a nun, he was furious.

He ran to the Roman Judges. "Lucy is a Christian," he said. The soldiers seized her. They threw her into a raging fire. But the flames did not hurt her. God protected her pure body.

So the soldiers plunged a sword into her heart.

And her pure soul went straight to Heaven.

Her Feast is December 13th.

St. Margaret Mary

OF THE SACRED HEART

We all know how much God loves us. He created us out of nothing. He died for our sakes. He stays with us in the Blessed Sacrament.

But men and women forget God so quickly.

He asks them to love Him. Instead they love all kinds of sinful and silly things.

Once upon a time, there was a very holy nun named Sister Margaret Mary.

She loved Our dear Lord with all her heart. She was sorry that everyone did not love Him too.

One day He appeared to her. He showed her His Sacred Heart.

"Behold the Heart that has loved men so much," He said. And He asked her to tell others about His love for them.

So Margaret Mary told everyone about the Sacred Heart.

She loved Jesus Christ with all her heart herself She brought millions to love Him too.

She is the saint of Sacred Heart of Jesus.

Her Feast is October 16th.

St. Martha

JESUS' FRIEND

Often our dear Lord was tired.

Often He grew weary when wicked men hated Him and tried to capture Him.

He would then go for a visit to His friends.

His friends were Lazarus and Mary and Martha.

They had a sweet and peaceful house in Bethany, not far from Jerusalem.

When He came to this house, He was happy.

Lazarus talked to Him. Mary sat at His feet and listened and loved Him.

But Martha was a busy little housekeeper.

She prepared the meals for our dear Lord.

When Lazarus, their brother, died, she and Mary sent for Jesus. All they said was, "The man You love is sick."

Jesus came Himself. In a wonderful miracle, He raised Lazarus from the dead. He gave their brother back to his sisters, Mary and Martha.

Martha was present on Calvary when Jesus died.

She helped prepare His body for burial.

She saw Him after He rose on Easter Sunday.

Later she and her brother and sister went to France. They told the French about Jesus. Many of the Frenchmen and women believed and became Christians.

Her Feast is July 29th.

St. Mary Magdalene

THE FORGIVEN ONE

Once upon a time, Mary Magdalene was a great sinner.

You see, she was very beautiful. So people paid her compliments. They ran after her and made her vain. She forgot that God gave her all her beauty. She loved rich clothes and fine jewels too much. She wanted to be popular at all costs.

So she sinned. And she was very unhappy.

Then one day, she saw Jesus, Our Lord.

He looked at her and showed her how sorry He was about her sin.

Right away, she knew how ugly sin was. She followed Jesus into the house of some rich men. Though they laughed at her, she knelt at His feet. She washed His feet with tears. She wiped them with her hair. She covered them with perfume.

She did this to show how sorry she was.

From that time on, she loved only Our Lord. She did not sin again. On Calvary, she stayed with Him until He died. After His resurrection, He showed Himself to her.

Then, when He rose into Heaven, Mary Magdalene ran off into the desert. She wanted to spend all her time thinking of Him, praying to Him, and loving Him with all her heart.

Her Feast is July 22nd.

St. Monica

MOTHER OF SAINT AUGUSTINE

Monica was a lovely young Roman girl.

She was wonderfully pure and good. She loved Jesus very much.

But her father loved money and power.

So he made her marry a young Roman who was very rich. Monica worried about her dear husband. She prayed hard that he would become a Catholic. She set him a good example. And a year before he died, he asked to be baptized.

But Augustine, her son, was her real worry.

Like his father, he did not care for the Catholic faith, and he led a wild and wicked life.

"I wish you would stop praying for me," he told her. But Monica prayed and prayed.

"Don't worry," a holy priest told her, "your son cannot be lost, not after all your prayers and tears."

So Monica followed Augustine to Rome. To her joy, she found that he had completely changed his life. He was a Catholic. He had given up his sins and his evil companions.

She thanked God. She died in peace knowing that her son was going to be a great saint and a great teacher and writer of Catholic truth.

Her Feast is August 27th.

St. Rita

SAINT OF THE IMPOSSIBLE

When Rita was a little girl, she wanted to be a Sister.

Instead, her Mother and Father made her marry a cruel, bad tempered husband.

But though he was unkind to her, Rita was a good wife. She had twin boys whom she loved very much.

But her husband had many enemies. One day, some of these men killed him. Her sons, now young men, were very angry.

"We will kill the men who murdered our Father," they cried. This is revenge and it is wrong.

Rita did not want them to commit mortal sin. She loved them. But she prayed to God to let them die rather than to commit a murder. Shortly after, God let them die. But first they confessed and received Holy Communion so that they went to Heaven.

Then Rita became an Augustinian nun.

During her life and after her death, she worked many miracles.

The Spaniards, because of her wonderful deeds, call her The Sweet Saint of the Impossible.

Her Feast is May 22nd.

St. Rose Of Lima

THE POOR LITTLE GIRL

This little girl is an American saint.

She was born in Lima in Peru. Columbus had discovered America less than one hundred years before.

Her name was really Isabel. But she was so beautiful that people called her Rose.

Her parents were poor. So little Rose became a maid servant.

Everybody noticed how beautiful she was. That made her afraid. Perhaps her good looks might lead her into sin. So she cut her lovely hair. She worked until her hands were rough. She wore old, unattractive clothes. She wanted her soul to be beautiful. Only God could see that.

Then she decided to become a Dominican nun.

So many people around her were sinful. Rose wanted to do penance for their sins. She lived in a little hut. She slept on the floor. She begged God to forgive sinners.

When the fleet of her country's enemies attacked Peru, her prayers drove them away and saved her city.

When she died, all Peru wept for the little Rose they loved.

Her Feast is August 23rd.

St. Scholastica

THE BENEDICTINE

Saint Benedict was the first of the holy monks.

Saint Scholastica was his beloved sister.

He built monasteries for holy men. She built convents for holy women.

Those were evil days and were full of dangers for good women.

Bands of wicked soldiers roamed all over the world.

So Saint Scholastica built lovely convents. They were full of peace. Women came there and were safe.

Saint Benedict loved his sister very much.

One day, he sat and talked with her about God.

Night came and he said, "I must go back to my home."

"Please don't go," she said. For she knew she was going to die.

When her brother, Benedict, insisted upon leaving, she bowed her head and prayed.

Suddenly a great storm burst. The wind blew. The rain fell. The lightning flashed. Benedict could not go back. So all night long they sang together, they prayed together, they talked about God.

Three days later, Scholastica died. And Benedict saw her soul going up to heaven in the form of a pure, white dove.

Her Feast is February 10th.

St. Therese

THE LITTLE FLOWER

This little saint lived in our own times. She was a little French girl named Theresa Martin.

Even as a little girl, she wanted to belong to God alone. Since people said, "You are too young," she asked the Pope to let her be a sister. So she entered the convent when still a child.

She joined the Carmelites. She said, "I just want to love God. I want to do hard things for Him. I want to pray for priests and for sinners. I want to shine like a little candle before His altar."

Almost nobody knew about this little girl. But the minute she died, all the world seemed to hear about her. They read her story and loved her. Soldiers chose her as their patroness. She became the saint of French aviators. Priests asked her to take care of them. Catholic missions were helped with her prayers.

Before she died, she said: "After death, I will drop down from Heaven a shower of roses."

She did just that.

Theresa, the Little Flower of Jesus, has filled the world with her miracles.

Her Feast is October 1st.

St. Ursula

THE TEACHER

When Ursula was a little girl, she loved children very much. She therefore became a teacher.

Mothers and fathers sent their boys and girls to her.

She taught them how to be good. She told them about Jesus and Mary.

She had a fine school for them in England.

But terrible pagan armies came into England. They threatened to kill all Christians. So Ursula took her pupils and her other teachers and went with them to France.

But once again, she met peril.

The terrible Huns came with their armies. They hated Jesus Christ and they killed all Christians.

So they captured Ursula and her sweet young companions.

They asked Ursula to let them make slaves of the little boys and girls. Ursula refused.

They promised to let them all go free if they would give up Christ and the Catholic faith.

They all refused.

So the army of the Huns drew their swords. They pulled back their bows and arrows. They killed Ursula and all her companions. And like glorious martyrs they went straight to heaven.

Her Feast is October 21st.

St. Veronica

OF THE WAY OF THE CROSS

We only know of one important incident in the life of Saint Veronica.

This took place on the terrible day of our dear Lord's Passion.

Jesus was carrying His cross. All around Him the people were laughing and screaming. They were throwing mud in His face. They were spitting upon Him. They tripped Him and made Him fall.

Jesus looked around and saw no friends. Everyone seemed to hate Him.

Then Veronica came.

She just happened to be in the crowd.

She was timid and afraid, but she wanted to help Him.

So she took the veil off her head. She pushed the soldiers aside. She ran through the crowd. She came to Jesus. He had just fallen and He was too weak to stand up. Lovingly she wiped His face with her veil.

Jesus looked up gratefully. He thanked her with a smile. The soldiers pushed her away.

But when she got home and looked at her veil, she found a wonderful thing.

On the veil was a beautiful picture of Jesus. And Veronica kept that as long as she lived.

Her Feast is July 12th.

INDEX

PAGE